Georges Bernage

Photo taken by the Germans the 7th or the 8th June from the towers of Ardenne Abbey near Caen. The powerfull naval armada of the Allies was a terrible vision for the Germans!. (PK Woscidlo, coll. Heimdal.)

Overlord

At the Teheran Conference in December 1943, the Russians demanded a landing by the Western Allies in France to relieve the pressure on their struggle with the Axis troops, principally the German Army. On the Other hand, Stalin was not keen on a landing on the Balkans as proposed by Winston Churchill which would have had the effect of inserting troops of the Western Allies directly into the heart of Western Europe, which was contrary to the plans of the Soviet Union to exercise total control over that area. Two landings in France were proposed – Overlord in Normandy and Anvil in Provence, but because of a shortage of landing craft, the two operations could not be carried out simultaneously. The Normandy beaches had been chosen in May 1943 at the Trident Conference in Washington, in preference to those in the Pas de Calais, more difficult and vastly better defended. The initial plan was to land a first wave of five divisions between the Orne and Vire estuaries - two American including one airborne and three British, one of which would also be airborne. This, however, was judged insufficient especially in view of the limited amount of transport aircraft available. Finally at the end of January 1944, Eisenhower decided to increase the forces allotted to the operation – three other divisions were to be engaged in the landing area which was extended to include the beaches to the east of the Cotentin Peninsular.

Responsibility for the ground operations of Overlord and the campaign in Normandy was vested in 21st Army Group, This had been formed in July 1943 and placed under the command of Sir Bernard Paget who had previously been in charge of Home Forces in Great Britain. Originally this army group only had British and Canadian units under command. During the preparations for Operation Overlord, however, the ground forces of the First American Army were placed under its command and the commander-in-chief was also given joint responsibility for the air and naval forced engaged in Operation Overlord. Paget, however was unknown to the public and had to be replaced by a « star », and to his great disappointment, he was sent to the Middle East as General in Charge at the end of 1943. He was replaced by General Montgomery who had made his name in the Desert War.

*Thus Sir Bernard Law Montgomery's **21st Army Group** had Lt-Gen. Omar Bradley's First US Army under its command which fielded two infantry divisions plus two airborne in the first wave, and the British Second Army which was involved with the sector under discussion here.*

So, the units of First US Army landed west of Port-en-Bessin, mainly in the Cotentin Peninsula, and the units of Second British Army east of Port-en-Bessin.

The last hours

By the end of May 1944, thousands of troops had been assembled on the south coast of England to wait for D-Day. The intensive training during the previous months had ratcheted up the tension. The officers had studied their objectives on coded maps and were extremely well informed with the aid of aerial photographs and intelligence supplied by the Resistance. Preparations had been intensive, everything had been examined and checked. Never before had such an operation been planned with such attention to detail. The stakes were far too high.

1. *Gosport on 3 June 1944. This reportage by Sgt. Mapham shows C Squadron of 13/18th Hussars in the process of loading. The Sherman tanks are reversing on board LCT 610. To enable them to find their right position during loading the number of the correct LCT has been marked on the sides of the vehicles. (IWM.)*

2. *One Sherman boarding on LCT 610. (IWM.)*

3. *Little far away, an armoured bulldozer D-7 going aboard LCT 789. (IWM.)*

4. *Aboard LCT 610 we find also elements of the 1st South Lancashires (8th Brigade, 3rd Division) and beach group elements. (IWM.)*

General Dwight D.Eisenhower
Commandant suprême
du Corps Expéditionnaire Allié

UTAH

Lieutenant General
L. Collins
VII US Corps

A

Lieutenant General
Omar Bradley
First US Army

OMAHA

Lieutenant General
L.T. Gerow
V US Corps

Major General
R.D. Barton
4th Infantry Division

Major General
R. Huebner
1st Infantry Division

Major General
H. Gerhardt
29th Infantry Division

Utah Beach

Omaha B

Ste-Mère-Eglise

Major General
M. B. Ridgway
82nd Airborne Division

Ste-Marie-du-Mont

Major General
M.D. Taylor
101st Airborne Division

L O R D

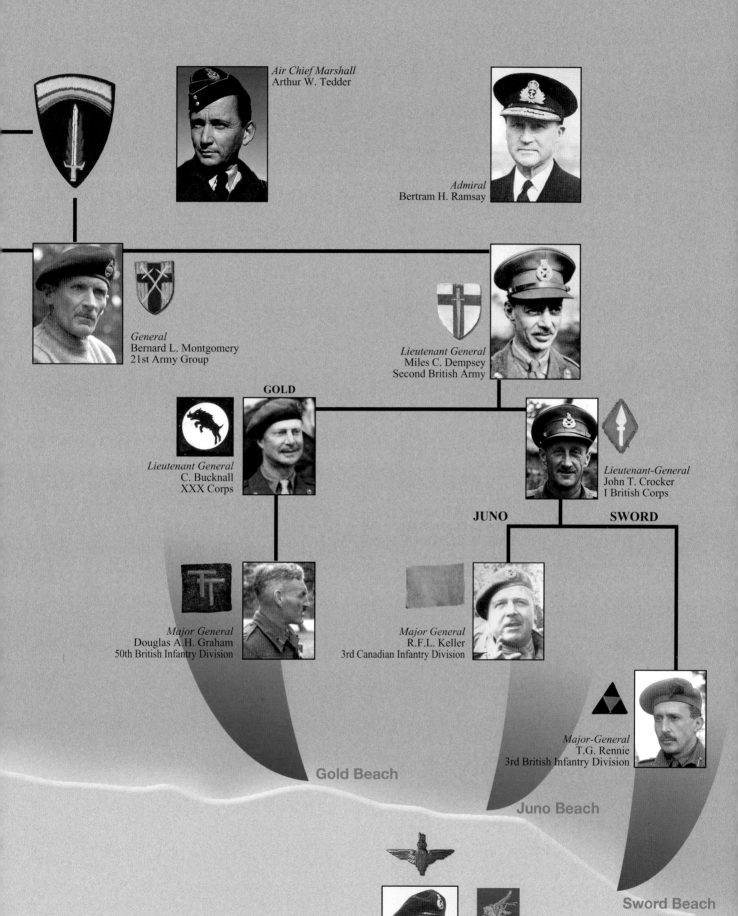

Air Chief Marshall
Arthur W. Tedder

Admiral
Bertram H. Ramsay

General
Bernard L. Montgomery
21st Army Group

Lieutenant General
Miles C. Dempsey
Second British Army

GOLD

Lieutenant General
C. Bucknall
XXX Corps

Lieutenant-General
John T. Crocker
I British Corps

JUNO

SWORD

Major General
Douglas A.H. Graham
50th British Infantry Division

Major General
R.F.L. Keller
3rd Canadian Infantry Division

Major-General
T.G. Rennie
3rd British Infantry Division

Gold Beach

Juno Beach

Sword Beach

Major-General
Richard N. Gale
6th Airborne Division

**PEGASUS BRIDGE
RANVILLE**

1

UTAH BEACH

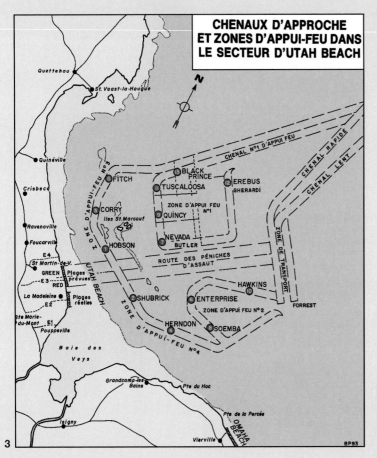

CHENAUX D'APPROCHE ET ZONES D'APPUI-FEU DANS LE SECTEUR D'UTAH BEACH

3

BP93

At dawn on D-day, the biggest armada ever was on its way to the Normandy coast. Soldiers and sailors were tightly squeezed in the ships, and sometimes had been so for several days. Some units, like U.S.S. Nevada, Erebus, Tuscaloosa and Quincy, H.M.S. Hawkins, Enterprise and Black Prince, based in Northern Ireland, had sailed from Belfast at 10.30 on 3 June.

1. All kinds of shipping advance coastwards in long lines, in prear-ranged channels, in a remarkably slick performance for such a com-plex organization. The barrage balloons were used to protect the fleet against possible German air attack. (US Navy.)

2. On this other aerial view of Utah Beach, the coast can be seen distinctly to bend round in the distance (to the south) towards the Baie des Veys. (US Air Force.)

3. Map showing the approach channels and fire support zones oppo-site Utah Beach. (Map by B. Paich/Heimdal.)

2

The 4th Division was substantially reinforced for the landing with other units, including the tanks of the 70th Tank Battalion (in the first wave), the tank destroyers of the 801st TD Battalion (SP) (from 9 to 13 June), the artillery batteries of the 13th FA Obsn Bn, Battery B of the 980th FA Bn (155 mm guns), Battery B of the 65th Armored Field Artillery Battalion, the 915th FA Bn (105 mm guns – a unit detached from the 90th Division – all its artillery units were attached to the 4th Division from 6 to 8 June). Antiaircraft units were also attached to the 4th Division: the 377th AAA AW Bn as of 14 June and Battery B, 453d AAA Aw Bn. Here we see medics belonging to a medical company coming ashore. (DAVA/Heimdal.)

4th Infantry Division

At **04.30**, four men armed only with knives swam up to the creeks of the Saint Marcouf islands, a tiny archipelago whose two main islands stood immediately opposite the planned landing zone. There were no Germans there.

A quarter of an hour after this first capture, at **05.45**, the invasion fleet was approaching the coast. The warships of Task Force 125 then opened fire to knock out the German defenses. USS Nevada's target was the Azeville battery, while Erebus took aim at La Pernelle, Tuscaloosa and Quincy Mont Coquerel and Saint-Marcouf/Crisbecq, Hawking Saint-Martin-de-Varreville (already destroyed by aerial bombardment), Black Prince engaged Morsalines and Enterprise the landing zone. The sloop Soemba concentrated its attack on the beach defenses. A few minutes later, 276 Marauders of the 9th US Air Force dropped 4,404 tons of bombs on seven targets from Wn 3 to Wn 10 with devastating results. The strong-

points were very badly hit and all telephone connections between German strongpoints were cut off. Lieutenant Colonel Keil could no longer give orders beyond his command post and so was unable to organize a coordinated defense. Cut off from each other, the survivors had to fend for themselves.

However, the landing fleet failed to arrive at its planned destination. In the unusual currents along the eastern coast of the Cotentin, producing a kind of "alternative tide", the ships had drifted off course to the south on the rising tide, with a stronger and shorter current. Instead of facing Wn 8 and StP 9, they were within sight of Lieutenant Jahnke's Wn 5, or what was left of it. But this navigational error turned out to be a blessing in disguise as the landing took place 2.5km (1.5mi) further south in a less exposed area almost out of range of the Saint Marcouf and Azeville batteries.

Utah Beach

1. As infantrymen clamber over the dunes on their way inland, others shelter behind the antitank wall awaiting orders to do likewise. This wall is still standing in 2004. (NA and E.G./Heimdal.)

2. The medics continue treating the wounded on the beach. In the background, infantrymen can be seen in foxholes they have dug in the sand. (D.F./Heimdal.)

3. This photo shows one side to the effects of the bombardments. A German soldier has been "buried" in the sand dune and is struggling to pull free. (D.F./Heimdal.)

From **06.20 to 06.40,** P-47 Thunderbolts carried out a rocket attack on the shore batteries to finish the job of silencing them. At **06.40,** twenty LCVPs brought in the first wave of 8th RCT, F and E Companies to the left at Uncle Red, and C and B Companies to the right, at Tare Green ten minutes later. About 300m (330yds) from the beach, the company commanders fired special smoke projectiles to request the ships to lengthen their range. Brigadier General Theodore Roosevelt came ashore at Uncle Red with the first wave. 70th Tank Battalion followed closely behind with its DD tanks. In view of the navigational error, General Roosevelt dispatched a recce party inland after Wn 5 had been taken rather easily. He located the causeway leading inland, Exit 2 towards Sainte-Marie-du-Mont. As things were going pretty well, the decision to press on in this sector was upheld.

The 237th Engineer Battalion cleared the beach and made breaches in the antitank wall. Within an hour the way was clear. At **08.00** Colonel Van Fleet's 8th Infantry Regiment and 3rd Battalion, 22nd Infantry Regiment had all come ashore. The rest of 22nd Infantry had landed by 10.00 as 8th Infantry Regiment advanced inland. Its 1st Battalion moved forward to the right towards La Madeleine and Wn 7, and further north to Exit 3 on its way to Audouville-la-Hubert.

Brigadier General Theodore Roosevelt

The son of President Theodore Roosevelt, he was born in 1887. He was a frail, poor-sighted young man who nevertheless fought with great courage with 1st Infantry Division during World War I. He later wrote books and entered politics. He joined the army again in 1941, and saw action in north Africa and Sicily. He insisted on joining the first assault waves armed with no more than his .45 colt and walking-stick... He landed in Corsica, then joined 4th Infantry Division, persuading General Barton to let him land with the first wave in Normandy. His considerable experience and bravery ensured success at Utah Beach and earned him a Medal of Honor. On July 12, 1944, having been promised command of 90th Infantry Division, he faced a counter-attack by 17. SS-Panzergrenadier-Division "Götz von Berlichingen" near Carentan. So intense was the battle that he died of a heart attack in a school playground at Méautis, at the age of 57. He was buried at the US cemetery at Colleville-sur-Mer in "D" square facing out to sea. Another Roosevelt is buried alongside him - his brother, a pilot killed during the Great War and who was brought here for them to lie side by side.

The Germans were demoralized and did not put up much of a fight. In the center, the next battalion (3/8) proceeded to Exit 2, heading for Sainte-Marie-du-Mont. Meanwhile 2/8 turned south to Wn 2 (La Petite Dune) before veering westwards via the short causeway leading to Exit 1, and on to Pouppeville, arriving at 12.00.

4. *In this photo, taken in the sand dunes at Utah Beach, we see the 4th Division commanders in discussion: Brigadier General Roosevelt, without his helmet (as seen by Sergeant Liska), and Major General Barton. Brig. Gen. Roosevelt came ashore with E Company in the first wave. (Heimdal.)*

5. *Sherman tanks of the C/70th Tank Battalion, with their hoods protecting their engine grilles against the sea, lend support to the landing troops. (NA/Heimdal.)*

6. *G.I.'s marching inland whith Machine gun. (Heimdal.)*

1. American paratrooper running towards the church at Sainte-Mère-Église, covered by one of his comrades. (NA/Heimdal).

2. Badge of 82nd Airborne Division.

3. American paratroop's metal insignia.

3

4

82nd Airborne Division

This airborne division landed with plenty of experience behind it. It was originally an infantry division and as such had taken part in the Great War. Its name "All American" refers to the fact that the men were drawn from all the states of the Union. After being reformed in May 1942, on August 16, 1942 the personnel of 82nd Infantry Division was split in two to form two airborne divisions: 82nd "All American" Airborne Division and 101st "Screaming Eagles" Airborne Division. The 82nd was sent to Morocco on May 10, 1943 for action in Tunisia. It was later dropped over Sicily on July 10, 1943 and over Italy, near Salerno, on September 13, 1943. The division arrived in Liverpool on April 22, 1944 to play its part in Operation Overlord.

On June 6, 1944, the divisional commander was Major General Matthew Ridgway, in charge of three parachute infantry regiments (505th, 507th and 508th PIR), one airlanding regiment (325th Glider Infantry Regiment), artillery (319th Glider Artillery Battalion to support 508th PIR, 320th Artillery Battalion to support 507th PIR, and 456th Parachute Artillery Battalion to support 505th PIR).

While 101st Airborne Division was dropped to the west of the Utah Beach landing sector to open up the beach exits for 4th Infantry Division, 82nd Airborne Division came down further inland and northwest of 101st Airborne.

This division had a number of assignments:

- to capture and hold Sainte-Mère-Église, an important crossroads on Highway 13; this was the mission of 505th PIR (2,208 men) which further had to mark out LZ W (at Les Forges) for the incoming gliders, also capture and hold two bridges over the Merderet (at La Fière and Chef-du-Pont);

- 507th PIR (1,936 men) was to establish a defensive front to the west of the Merderet and assist 505th PIR in defending the bridges;

- 508th PIR (2,183 men) was to capture and demolish the bridges at Beuzeville, prepare to advance towards the Douve River, and make up a reserve battalion.

A hectic night at Sainte-Mère-Église

Elements of IR 1058 were based in this small Cotentin town. The population was in a state of expectation following regular bombing raids along the coast over the previous few days. On this June 5, 1944, at around eleven pm, the clear night - the moon was full - was lit up by a fire (we shall never know what caused it) at the house of Julia Pommier ("3" on the plan). The alarm bell was ringing as the people formed a chain to put out the fire. A first aircraft formation then flew over the town, followed by another, flying lower. By this time it was one in the

5

4. Dummy paratrooper hanging from the church bell tower in honor of John Steele. (Heimdal photo).

5. The main street at Sainte-Mère-Église (looking northwards, the church is on the right), in June 1944; the place has remained completely unchanged. (Photo, B.Piper/Heimdal).

6. The church at Saint-Mère-Église with the pump used during the night of June 5-6, 1944 to fight the fire at Julie Pommier's house. (Heimdal photo).

7. Center of Sainte-Mère-Église, on the night of June 5-6, 1944. René Jamard and Jules Lemenicier were killed during the battle. (Heimdal plan).

6

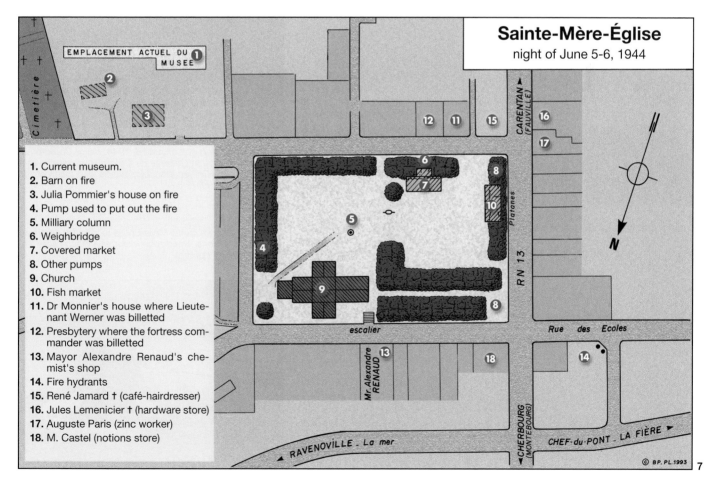

Sainte-Mère-Église
night of June 5-6, 1944

1. Current museum.
2. Barn on fire
3. Julia Pommier's house on fire
4. Pump used to put out the fire
5. Milliary column
6. Weighbridge
7. Covered market
8. Other pumps
9. Church
10. Fish market
11. Dr Monnier's house where Lieutenant Werner was billetted
12. Presbytery where the fortress commander was billetted
13. Mayor Alexandre Renaud's chemist's shop
14. Fire hydrants
15. René Jamard † (café-hairdresser)
16. Jules Lemenicier † (hardware store)
17. Auguste Paris (zinc worker)
18. M. Castel (notions store)

7

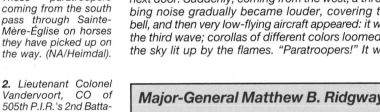

1. *Afternoon of June 7. These paratroopers coming from the south pass through Sainte-Mère-Église on horses they have picked up on the way. (NA/Heimdal).*

morning and the fire had spread to the wooden barn next door. Suddenly, coming from the west, a throbbing noise gradually became louder, covering the bell, and then very low-flying aircraft appeared: it was the third wave; corollas of different colors loomed in the sky lit up by the flames. "Paratroopers!" It was

2. *Lieutenant Colonel Vandervoort, CO of 505th P.I.R.'s 2nd Battalion, walking with a crutch, having injured his left ankle. (NA/ Heimdal).*

3. *Major General M.B. Ridgway. (US Army).*

Major-General Matthew B. Ridgway

He was born at Fort Monroe, Virginia on March 3, 1895 and finished at the US Military Academy in April 1917. He held several commands overseas, in China, in the Philippines and in Nicaragua. Upon graduating from Staff College, he was appointed to the general staff, where he remained until January 1942. On June 26, 1942, he was given command of 82nd Infantry Division which became an airborne division. He commanded the division in action in north Africa, Sicily and Italy. For Overlord, he preferred to join the airdrop with his men rather than come in by glider. He landed in a field west of Sainte-Mère-Église. In August 1944, he was put in command of XVIII Airborne Corps which he led into battle in the Ardennes, during the Rhine crossing, in the Ruhr pocket and on the Elbe until the Americans linked up with the Soviets on May 2, 1945. After the war, he became commander-in-chief in the Mediterranean. He commanded US Eighth Army in Korea in 1950 and became commander-in-chief in Korea on April 11, 1951. In May 1952, he succeeded Dwight D. Eisenhower as commander-in-chief of the Allied Forces in Europe. He was made US Army chief-of-staff on August 15, 1953 and retired on June 30, 1955 at the end of a brilliant career. He died on July 26, 1993 at the age of 98.

4. *During the afternoon of June 6, 1944, Major Crandell set up a field hospital at Château de Colombières, south-east of Sainte-Mère-Église; this color photo was taken at the time. (Heimdal coll.).*

5. *The museum at Sainte-Mère-Église recalls the American airborne operations. The display includes a Waco glider and a C.47. (Heimdal photo).*

00.15 (British time, 01.15 French time). 506th PIR dropped two sticks over the town. It was total chaos as the Germans opened fire on the paratroops. On Mayor Alexandre Renaud's recommendation, the civilians dived for cover. A third stick (of 505th PIR's Company "F") arrived twenty minutes later; Sergeant

Ray was killed on hitting the ground by a burst of machine-gun fire and Pfc Blankenship came down straight into the blazing house. Shearer fell into a tree and was killed instantly, while a dozen bodies were left hanging from the trees. Private John Steele was wounded by shrapnel in the left foot and drifted towards the bell tower, snarling his parachute on it. At the time, Rudolf May, a German soldier, was in the bell tower but did not fire at John Steele for fear of being spotted, for he had seen down below his buddy Alfons Jakl killed by an American paratrooper as he landed. John Steele was in fact captured by the Germans but escaped a few days later. Finally, the German soldiers mustered in three ranks on the square and left the village uncertain as to what was going on, withdrawing to Château de Fauville (a kilometer to the south). Soon, American paratroops, particularly I Company of 505th PIR, joined up to the east of the village before entering it. The village was invested by 505th PIR's 3rd Battalion (3/505) which landed at DZ O to the west at 02.03. An hour later, Lieutenant-Colonel Krause had gathered 158 men with whom he set about capturing Sainte-Mère-Église, a mission accomplished at five. The men of this regiment's 2nd Battalion (2/505) landed on Norman soil at the earlier time of 00.51. Their CO, Lieutenant-Colonel Vandervoort, sustained an injury to the left ankle. His men carried him off, leaning on his rifle, in a folding munitions trailer. His battalion was to provide protection for Sainte-Mère-Église 2km (1mi) to the north, by establishing itself at Neuville-au-Plain. Vandervoort moved on to Sainte-Mère-Église at 10.00, by which time the Germans had already launched their counter-attacks. The village was the scene of a fierce battle, with a number of civilian casualties. The German attacks, none of them successful, conti-

nued until late afternoon. The little village of Sainte-Mère-Église had just found a place in the history books.

La Fière and the Merderet River

Further west, the way forward was blocked by the inundated Merderet valley. There were several bridges across it, including one at La Fière. North-west of this valley, 507th PIR carried out the most disastrous air-drop that night at around 02.30, when many paratroopers were scattered and landed in the marshes, with most of their equipment lost as well. However, while 1/505's objective was the **La Fière bridge**, some of 507th PIR assembled north of La Fière in support of 1/505. As for 508th PIR, the men were scattered all over the area and only Lieutenant-Colonel Shanley was able to capture a strongpoint, near Hill 30. The capture of the La Fière bridge was the task of 505th PIR's A Company, which was to link up with the forces of 507th PIR on the west bank. This objective was achieved at 06.00, and the assault was launched an hour later. General Gavin arrived with reinforcements at about 08.30. The bridge and causeway were captured and secured two hours later. Towards noon, came a German counter-attack from the west bank with two Panzer-Abteilung 100 tanks. Both tanks were knocked out. The bridge was victoriously held, and became the key to further progress westward to Pont-l'Abbé, Saint-Sauveur-le-Vicomte and Barneville.

6. At Saint-Marcouf, north-east of Sainte-Mère-Église, an officer of 101st Airborne listens to information from a civilian. The Americans were often mistrustful, having been warned to watch out for "collaborators". (DAVA/Heimdal).

1. Germans watching the beach from a range-finding post. (BA.)

2. American RCT landing sectors at Omaha Beach. (Heimdal.)

3. This is how US troops experienced the D-Day assault on Omaha Beach… (Heimdal coll.)

4. … and this is how the war correspondents captured the moment for posterity. (NA/Heimdal.)

Background photograph: *Omaha Beach seen from where the American cemetery now stands, between what were strongpoints Wn 64 and (on the right) Wn 62. Wn 62 caused heavy losses among the landing troops. (G. Bernage/ Heimdal photo.)*

"Bloody Omaha"

05.50, June 6. The destroyers of Force O opened fire on the coastline: USS Satterlee pounded the defenses at Pointe du Hoc. The Texas opened fire on the defenses of Dog sector, the Arkansas attacked the D3 exit, the Georges Leygues (of the Free French Naval Forces) and the Tanat Side took aim at E1 (on Easy), etc. But most of their shells fell a mile inland, killing a few cows.

06.00. The northwesterly wind had dropped, although still with gusts of up to 18 knots. The waves were three to six feet high. In the small assault craft, the men were weak with seasickness as they approached the coast. Then 480 B-24 bombers carrying 1,285 tons of bombs passed overhead. But owing to low cloud, the planes dropped their bombs too far inland. The mission was a total failure, with one bomb falling just behind Wn 62, and all the rest further back in the fields. The German positions remained intact whereas the troops coming ashore thought they had been wiped out …

Opposite where the US cemetery now stands, the Sherman DD (amphibious) tanks of 741st Tank Battalion (116th RCT, 1st Div.) began to leave their twelve LCTs at 05.35. German shells soon started to rain on the LCTs. In heavy seas, only two DD tanks made it to the beach, the others foundered or their engines were flooded. When four tanks were brought directly onto the beach, after their LCT had been damaged by shellfire, opposite Vierville (Dog sector), Captain Elder and Lieutenant Rockwell decided, in view of the rough sea, to bring all 743rd Tank Battalion's DD tanks right up to the beach in their LCTs.

06.25. Squad 14 of the Special Engineer Task Force arrived off Easy Red opposite the Ruquet valley; the beach was deserted, they were early. Their LCM was hit by a shell, and they were all killed or wounded, the first Americans to die at Omaha Beach…

06.30. The leading wave arrived on the beach. The assault force was divided between the two divisions. To the east, 1st Infantry Division was committed with 116th RCT opposite Saint-Laurent and Colleville (Easy and Fox). To the west, 29th Infantry Division was committed with 16th RCT opposite Dog. However the undercurrents at Omaha Beach were very powerful at that time; on the rising tide, a side current runs all along the coastline in an eastward direction, reaching 2.7 knots 5 miles (8km) out to sea. The Rangers landing at Pointe du Hoc had to face the same problem but managed to reset their course in time. Off Omaha Beach, the early morning mist and smoke from the naval guns made it impossible to look for landmarks on the shore. The landing craft all drifted eastwards and the infantry came ashore opposite different targets from those for which they had been prepared. Nobody at all landed in some sectors, whilst elsew-

here several companies were mixed up together as they came in at the same point. All this created a great deal of confusion further aggravated by the fierceness of the battle.

At Wn 62, opposite Fox Green, Captain Frerking was range-finding for the 105mm gun battery positioned at Houtteville. Beside him, Corporal Heinrich Severloh was firing an MG 42 machine-gun at a rate of 1,500 rounds a minute. It was 06.30. The artificial fog had lifted, revealing the Allied fleet 8 or 10 km (5-6mi) offshore. At Wn 62 there were eight artillerymen and eighteen infantrymen. Slightly to Frerking's left, Corporal Severloh saw American soldiers coming ashore just 800 meters away. He was preparing to follow the order issued by Captain Frerking: "When they are up to their knees in water, you must fire, and not until then!" So Severloh fired at the two columns of soldiers already in the water, coming down the side ramps of a troop transport vessel. The first man in each column fell, then the others behind him. More followed, and when they were up to their knees in water Severloh opened fire again. From Wn 62, on the right, Franz Gockel of 716th Infantry was also causing devastating losses to the assault troops with his Polish-built Bren gun. Also, again on Captain Frerking's instructions, radio operators Sossna and Gebauer sent orders to the artillery at the Houtteville battery (1./AR 352) and their shells exploded on the beach. Altogether by the end of his battle with the landing forces, Severloh had fired about 12,000 rounds with his MG 42 and 300 to 400 with his carbine.

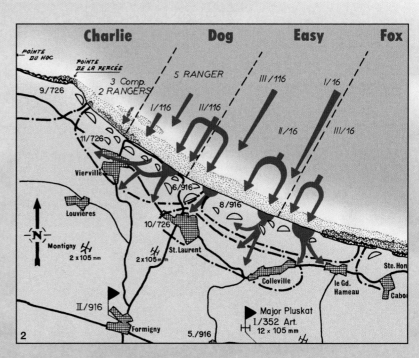

Omaha Beach

The best series of photos of the landings in Omaha Beach were taken by a Coast Guard photographer from an LCVP, four of which are reproduced here.

1. The LCVP approaches the coast. Each assault company was transported either by 6 LCVP's or 6 LCA's, each of which could carry thirty men. There is a lieutenant of the 1st Inf. Div. in the front on the left who was the platoon commander. The mens' rifles were protected by plastic covers. They were exhausted by the crossing, wracked by seasickness and crowded together they suffered from cramp, cold and were drenched through by the waves that broke over them, their feet in a mixture of vomit and seawater.

2. The approach to the beach. One can see the beach obstacles uncovered by the low tide and the smoke-covered ridge in the background.

On the left another LCVP.(PA 26-17), hit by a German shell and emitting a plume pf smoke.

3. H-Hour on Easy Red. The landing craft piloted by the Coast Guards landed their soldiers from the 16th RCT between WN62 (left) and WN64 (right) facing the plateau where, after the war, the US cemetery was laid out. We can see in front the landing craft PA 26-18 and PA 26-19 whose men were advancing through the waist deep water.

4. The LCVP from which these photos were taken has just dropped off its infantrymen. One can recognise it from the loop of cable or rope seen in the first photo on the left). On front among the obstacles the men of E/16th and E/116th are all jumbled up have been stopped by the machine-guns of WN62 further to the left. In the centre distance, tank no. 9 of the 741st Tank Battalion can be made out.

(photos NA/coll. Heimdal)

3

4

Omaha Beach

Easy Red. Robert Capa.

0630. Robert Capa landed with the first assault wave " between the grotesque shapes of steel obstacles....a narrow strip of sand covered by smoke, our Europe, Easy Red Beach". Facing WN62, a terrible place. He forced his way through the water amid a hail of bullets and managed to take 106 photos, most of which were ruined during development. Only ten were rescued, exceptional documents snapped at H Hour and here are five of them.

1. Capa quickly turned and took this soldier stretched out in the water in the middle of the obstacles. Tanks were coming ashore and the beach obstacles offered the only cover from the enemy gunfire coming from WN62.

2. This slightly sharper photo shows a group of soldiers huddling around a Czech Hedgehog.

3. There were others a little further away amid the obstacles.

4. Capa then went on to take several shots in the direction the fire was coming from. This photo shows men from either Company E or F on the 116th RCT struggling towards the start of the beach, having left their LCVP.

3

5. *They sheltered behind some DD tanks which had been dropped off, one of which had brewed up.*
(NA/Coll Heimdal).

4

5

1. *Aid men installed themselves by the shingle bank in the middle of the debris : here they are giving a transfusion.*

2. *Further on a doctor captain and other medical orderlies are also giving a transfusion to a wounded man covered by a blanket. His head is resting on a life belt used as a pillow.*

Fox Red.

At Colleville-sur-Mer, below the hamlet of Cabourg and WN60, the 6th Naval Beach Battalion set up a first aid post sheltered by the chalk cliff and right below the German defended position, at circa 0720. The war correspondent Taylor took a set of exceptional shots which were most evocative of the horrors experienced on Omaha beach. Printed here are a dozen of the photos showing men of the 3rd. Battalion of the 16th RCT. (1st Inf. Div.).

3. An orderly giving first aid to a wounded man whose expression is still marked by the terrors he has seen.

4. An orderly filling out the wound report card for a man with bandaged head.

5. Other wounded awaiting evacuation having received first aid. Three of them have suffered head wounds. Between 6 and 18 June, 11.25% of the wounds were to the head.

(DAVA, ETO-HQ-44 series 4778. Coll. Heimdal)

Fox Red.

Underneath WN60, Correspondent Taylor continued taking photos.

6. This is a close-up of a sailor still in shock. Between 6 and 28 June, the US Navy also suffered heavy losses ; 12 officers and 95 other ranks killed, 204 missing and 313 wounded. Most of the casualties were from the Naval Beach Battalions the units of Navy Engineers who had taken part in the clearing of obstacles.

7. This shot shows walking wound and others who had survived sinkings. One can see to the left the sailor in the preceding photo. The vertical cliff face was a landmark which can be seen later.

8. Taylor carried on his way and one can see here the backs of the soldiers in the previous shot.

9. Beside a body or a man seriously wounded, a not so serious casualty in the process of recovery.

10. Others were not so lucky, their bodies laid out on the shingle at the water's edge.

11. These men, armed with a heavy machine-gun are setting off westwards, probably to attack WN60.

12. The same place as it is today. From there one can see the entire beach as far as the Pointe de la Percée. (photo GB)

(Photos DAVA-ETO-HQ-44 series 4778. Coll Heimdal).

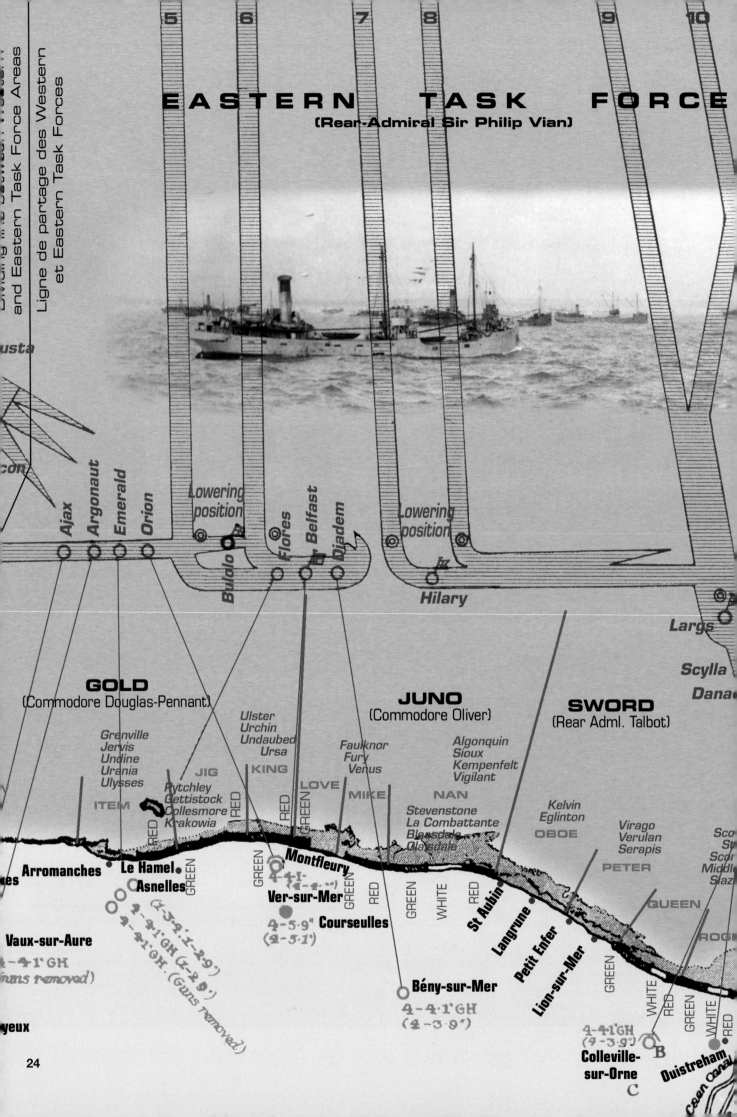

5 **6** **7** **8** **9** **10**

EASTERN TASK FORCE
(Rear-Admiral Sir Philip Vian)

Dividing line between Western
and Eastern Force Areas

Ligne de partage des Western
et Eastern Task Forces

usta

con

Ajax *Argonaut* *Emerald* *Orion*

*Lowering
position*

Bulolo

Flores

Belfast

Diadem

*Lowering
position*

Hilary

Largs

Scylla

Danae

GOLD
(Commodore Douglas-Pennant)

*Grenville
Jervis
Undine
Urania
Ulysses*

JIG

ITEM

*Pytchley
Gettistock
Collesmore
Krakowia*

*Ulster
Urchin
Undaubed
Ursa*

KING

RED

LOVE

RED

GREEN

*Faulknor
Fury
Venus*

MIKE

JUNO
(Commodore Oliver)

*Algonquin
Sioux
Kempenfelt
Vigilant*

NAN

*Stevenstone
La Combattante
Blaasdale
Glaisdale*

*Kelvin
Eglinton*

OBOE

SWORD
(Rear Adml. Talbot)

*Virago
Verulan
Serapis*

PETER

*Sco
St
Scor
Middle
Slaz*

Arromanches

Le Hamel
Asnelles

GREEN

Montfleury
4·4·I·
(4-4.⁰⁰)

Ver-sur-Mer

GREEN

4·5·9" **Courseulles**
(4-5.1")

GREEN

RED

GREEN

St Aubin

WHITE

RED

Langrune

QUEEN

Petit Enfer

Lion-sur-Mer

GREEN

ROG

Vaux-sur-Aure

4-4·1'GH
(ns removed)

(4-3.9.1-3.9")
4-41'GH (4-2.9")
4-41'GH. (Guns removed)

yeux

Bény-sur-Mer
4-4·1'GH
(4-3.9")

4-4·1'GH
(9-3.9")

B

**Colleville-
sur-Orne**

C

WHITE

RED

GREEN

WHITE

RED

Ouistreham

Caen Canal

24

PERATION « NEPTUNE »
Landing in Normandy
June, 1944
Bay of the Seine
PRE-ARRANGED
BOMBARDMENT

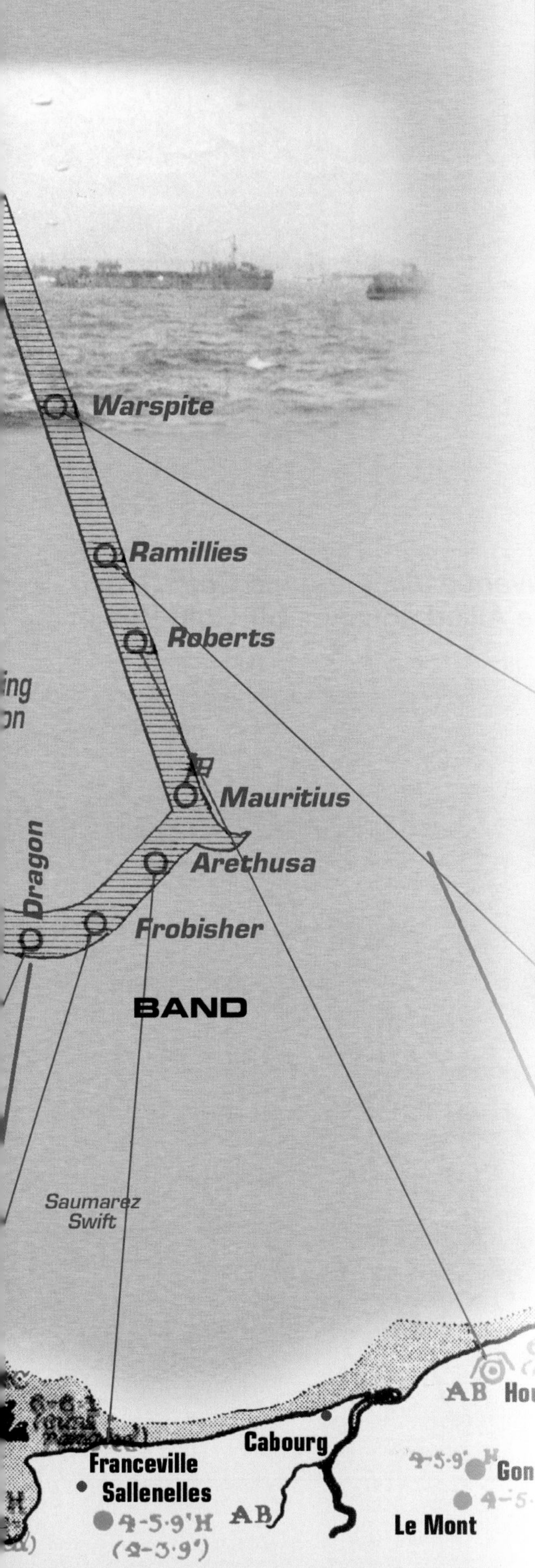

The Bombarding Force opens fire with its heavy guns on the German batteries.

H.M.S. Warspite fires on the Villerville battery.

H.M.S. Roberts fires on the Houlgate battery.

Warspite

Ramillies

Roberts

Mauritius

Arethusa

Dragon

Frobisher

BAND

Saumarez
Swift

Beneville

Benerville

AB Houlgate

Cabourg

Franceville
Sallenelles

4-5·9'H **Gonneville**

4-5·9'

4-5·9'H **AB**

(2-5·9')

Le Mont

Gold Beach

Royal Marines of the 47th RM Commando disembark from their LCAs on Jig Beach congested with the LCTs that brought in the special tanks. On the left, a bulldozer is pushing a truckload of fascines. (IWM.)

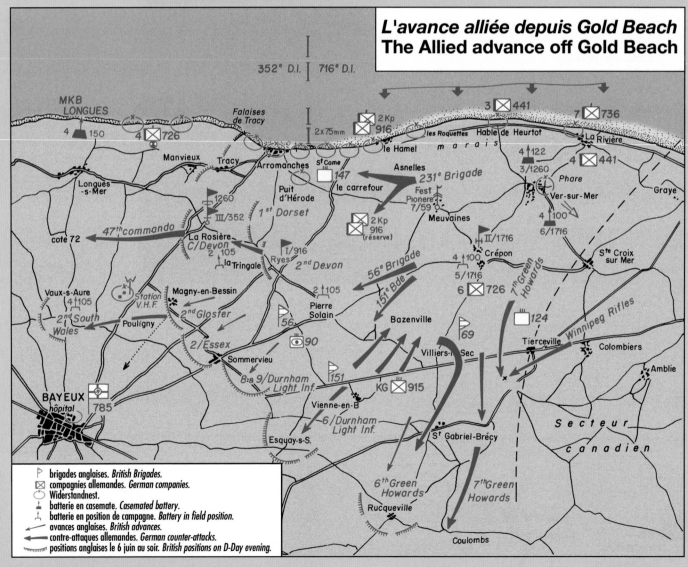

L'avance alliée depuis Gold Beach
The Allied advance off Gold Beach

352e D.I. 716e D.I.

MKB LONGUES

4 150   4 726   Falaises de Tracy   2x75mm   2 Kp 916   les Roquettes   Hable de Heurtot   3 441   7 736

Manvieux   Tracy   Arromanches   St Come   le Hamel   marais   La Rivière

Longues-s-Mer   1260   Puit d'Hérode   147   le carrefour   Asnelles   231e Brigade   Fest Pionere 7/59   Meuvaines   4 122   3/1260   4 441   Phare   Ver-sur-Mer   Graye

cote 72   47th commando   III/352   1st Dorset   2 Kp 916 (réserve)   II/1716   Crépon   4 100   6/1716   Ste Croix sur Mer

La Rosière   C/Devon   2 105   I/916   la Tringale   Ryes   2nd Devon   56e Brigade   4 100   5/1716   7th Green Howards

Vaux-s-Aure   4 105   Station V.H.F.   Magny-en-Bessin   2 105   151 Bde   6 726   Bazenville   124   Tierceville   Winnipeg Rifles   Colombiers

2nd South Wales   Pouligny   2nd Glosfer   Pierre Solain   56   69   Villiers-l- Sec   Amblie

2/Essex   Sommervieu   90   KG 915

BAYEUX   hôpital   785   8:a 9/Durnham Light Inf.   151   Vienne-en-B   St Gabriel-Brécy   Secteur canadien

6/Durnham Light Inf.

Esquay-s-S.   6th Green Howards   7th Green Howards

Rucqueville

Coulombs

brigades anglaises. British Brigades.
compagnies allemandes. German companies.
Widerstandnest.
batterie en casemate. Casemated battery.
batterie en position de campagne. Battery in field position.
avances anglaises. British advances.
contre-attaques allemandes. German counter-attacks.
positions anglaises le 6 juin au soir. British positions on D-Day evening.

CSM Hollis' Victoria Cross

On 6 June, Company Sergeant-Major Stanley Elton Hollis commanded a platoon of the 6th Green Howards D Company (commander Major Lofthouse). On that day, CSM Hollis distinguished himself twice to earn a rare and prestigious decoration, the Victoria Cross, the only one awarded in Normandy on 6 June 1944. His first action took place at the Mont-Fleury battery, where he cleared two pillboxes with a Sten Gun and grenades, thus helping to open up the road from the beach to Ver and protect his comrades' lives. Later, at Crépon, Major Lofthouse detailed him to clear part of the village. He entered a farm, spotted a German battery from a garden gate and attacked it with a PIAT, while all his men around him were hit. He contributed to the destruction of this battery and saved the lives of two of his men.

GOLD BEACH

The Gold Beach sector stretched for ten miles (16 km) but its entire western section consisted of cliffs overhanging the sea. However, this sector had a bay where an artificial harbor, codenamed Mulberry, was to be built and it also had a port of discharge at Port-en-Bessin. So these were vital objectives that were achieved from the only available beaches, at Asnelles (Jig Beach) and Ver-sur-Mer (King Beach), the principal objective for D-Day evening being the town of Bayeux, an important crossroads. The landing was carried out by the considerably reinforced 50th Northumbrian Division under Major General Graham. Thus, by D-Day evening, 25,000 men had been brought ashore on these two beaches.

The initial attack was carried out by two infantry brigades (the division had four brigades, specially for D-Day). In the east, on King Beach, the 69th Infantry Brigade committed the 6th Green Howards in front of Wn 35 held by a company of Russian volunteers at Le Hable de Heurtot, subsequent objectives being the Mont Fleury battery (3./HKA 1260) and the Mare Fontaine battery (Wn 32, 6./AR 1716), and then Crépon. In the west, on Jig Green (east of Asnelles), the 231st Infantry Brigade committed of the 1st Hampshires near Les Roquettes (1st Dorset) to seize Wn 36, and then fork off towards Hamel and Wn 37 in the seaside sector of Asnelles.

1. On 7 June, in the southern part of the village of Ver-sur-Mer, on the Crépon road, a British captain takes charge of two German prisoners belonging to a Flak unit. (IWM.)

2 and **3.** Today. A signpost to Crépon recalls one painted by the British on the house in this photo. (EG/Heimdal.)

Juno Beach

Bernières

1 and **2.** This pillbox, an element of strongpoint Wn 28 defended by 5./736 and housing a 5 cm KwK gun, was a thorn in the side of the Queen's Own Rifles, who lost 65 men on this beach. (APC.) The pillbox is still standing, and two monuments have been erected nearby, one dedicated to the

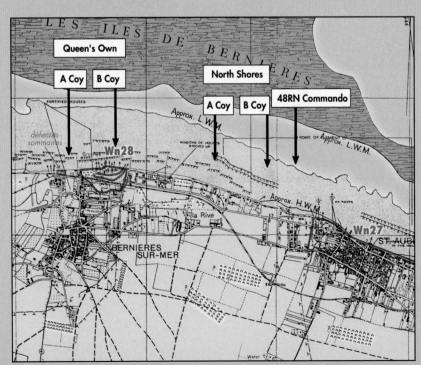

JUNO BEACH

6 June, 1944, the Canadian 3rd Infantry Division was to land along a vast sector of beaches codenamed Juno Beach. 7th Brigade was to come ashore in the west at Graye and Courseulles, and 8th Brigade in the east at Bernières and Saint-Aubin.

In the east of the Juno Beach sector, the 8th Brigade, commander Brigadier K.G. Blackader, was to attack along two lines. The Régiment de la Chaudière and the Queen's Own Rifles would land at Bernières-sur-Mer (Nan White). In the easternmost sector, the North Shore Regiment was to land at Saint-Aubin-sur-Mer (Nan Red) with support from the amphibious tanks of the Fort Garry Horse (Canadian 10th Armoured Regiment).

Queen's Own and the other to the Fort Garry Horse. A little further on, near a Tobruk, another has been erected in memory of the Regiment de la Chaudière. (EG/HDL.)

3. Another photo taken on the same spot that same day, showing a corporal of the Régiment de la Chaudière guarding German prisoners. (APC.)

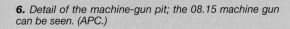

6. Detail of the machine-gun pit; the 08.15 machine gun can be seen. (APC.)

Passing in front of an AVRE of the 80th Assault Squadron, M. Grave pushing the cart and M. Martin wearing the beret, as described by Marcel Ouimet, are directed towards the beach accompanied by Sergeant Gagnon. (APC.)

1 and **2.** Nan-Red - Saint-Aubin. By the time the Royal Marines came ashore at Saint-Aubin at 08.43, the tide had come in, two LCI(S)s hitting mines placed on beach obstacles and sinking. They also came under fire from the 50 mm gun which had not yet been silenced. (IWM.) And today. (HDL.)

3

3. *This photograph was taken a little further west from the previous one: notice the voile panels and the smoke in the laniard. In the foreground can be seen one of the Centaur tanks lending support to the Royal Marines. (IWM.)*

Nan Red: Saint-Aubin

North Shore (New Brunswick) Regiment *was commanded by Lieutenant-Colonel D.B. Buell. It had been detailed to land at 07.55 at Saint-Aubin west, mop up the beach defenses (including a stout pocket of resistance), occupy the locality and form the Canadian division's eastern flank there. This regiment was to be accompanied by N° 48 RM Commando (British) which was to fork off eastwards behind the Canadians, from the positions taken by the North Shore Regt, in order to attack Langrune-sur-Mer. Meanwhile, the North Shores would head off due south towards Tailleville and the radar tracking station at Basly-Douvres, their final D-Day objective.*

6

4 *and* **5.** *Slightly further east, we come to Saint-Aubin and these two photos were taken from the concrete bunker housing the 50 mm guns (the muzzle can be seen on one of the pictures). It was in the middle of Wn 27 and covered the beach. The windows on the houses along the sea front have been partly walled up to leave the defending Germans with firing embrasures. After the fighting, the beach is cluttered with various debris including the wreck of a Thunderbolt which crashed on it. (Coll. Heimdal.)*

6. *The place has remained as it was, with the 50 cm gun still in its bunker. (EG/HDL.)*

1 and **2.** The 48 RM Commando landed at 08.43 on the eastern edge of Nan Red, on the boundary with Oboe Beach and the approaches to Saint-Aubin, under threat from the 50 mm gun positioned there. The landing took place at high tide over the beach obstacles. The unit's losses for the day totalled 50 %, three quarters of them on the beach. Here we see the 4th S.S. Brigade's HQ landing at 09.00 hours. The ramps are stiff and move up and down with the waves, causing some of the heavily burdened Royal Marines to slip. (IWM.)

3. The Royal Marines now head off towards Langrune with bicycles and towing heavily loaded trailers. However they came under mortar fire and had to take cover. (IWM.)

4. A little further on, before Langrune, civilians pass on information to Captain Wilmot, a 4th Special Service Brigade Intelligence Officer. This unit was detailed to take Langrune and then to head off east to Petit Enfer (Luc-sur-Mer) to link up with the 41 RM Commando. But both units were held up in front of their respective objectives. (IWM.)

Juno Beach

The Canadian landing

These wonderfull colour pictures were taken on D-Day at Bernières-sur-Mer where units of the Queen's Own (3rd Canadian Infantry Division) are landing.

1 and 2. Big ships (LSIs, APAs and AKAs) transport Landing Crafts to bring the men ashore. We see here such ships before the coast at Bernières-sur-Mer. (Photos Ken Bell/National Defence Library.)

3, 4 and **5.** On D-Day
long files of Canadian
soldiers are landing at
high tide and low tide
(with a wider beach). The
beach obstacles had
been put away.

(Photos Ken Bell/Natio-
nal Defence Images Li-
brary.)

SWORD BEACH

Leading the way in to Queen Beach came eight LCTs (LCTs 101 to 108) bringing DD tanks for 13th/18th Hussars. They were to stop 5,000 yards (c. 4.5 km) off the coast to launch their DD tanks at around **06.00 hours**, as day dawned in grey skies. It had been intended to launch them 7,000 yards out but in view of the heavy seas, this had not been possible. This was an unpleasant operation for the crews. The flotation skirts were raised, and they could see nothing from behind them, having to navigate coastwards by compass (it had to indicate 180°). Water came up almost to the top of the skirt and they had to use pumps to bale out the water they shipped, and progress was slower than planned in such rough seas. Out of the 40 DD tanks brought across, 34 were sent ashore, and 31 actually reached the beach.

Starting at **06.44**, the naval support pounded the coast with shellfire, adding to the din of the Bombarding Force which had opened fire over an hour earlier. Rocket salvoes screamed through the air, a reassuring sound for the seasick infantry packed in their LCAs since 05.30. Behind these frail craft came 18 LCTs (LCTs 272 to 283 and LCTs 331 to 336) carrying self-propelled guns for 7th Field Regiment R.A, 76th (Highland) Field Regiment R.A. and 33rd Field Regiment R.A. fired their shells at the coast. In each LCT, there were two self-propelled guns in the bows and two in the stern, with various vehicles in between.

07.20. Day had dawned. The landing at Sword Beach was scheduled about 90 minutes later than on the other beaches, the German defenses were partly intact and the men of Grenadier-Regiment 736 were emerging from the deluge of fire. 22nd Dragoons' flail tanks were the first to hit the beach along with their squads of engineers. The leading AVREs arrived at 07.25. These powerful tanks engaged the enemy positions, then 31 amphibious tanks of 13/18th Royal Hussars arrived in turn to silence the 50 and 75mm guns. A good job well done by both tanks and engineers.

At 07.30, twenty LCAs brought in the assault companies: in the west 1st South Lancashire A and C Companies to Queen White; in the east 2nd East Yorkshire A and C Companies to Queen Red. But they were all held up at the top of the beaches behind the antitank wall. Then a flail tank knocked out a 75mm gun that had just caused 200 casualties among the East Yorkshires.

The two assault battalions' other companies and the two LCIs bringing in the Frenchmen of n°4 Commando (the Kieffer Commando) came ashore in turn at 07.31. After sprinting up the beach Commando n°4 opened a breach in the barbed wire. At 07.55, it was in the ruins of a holiday camp and headed off towards Ouistreham. At 08.42, LCI 501 hit the beach, the ramp was lowered, and to the sound of the bagpipes of Piper Bill Millin accompanying his commanding officer, Lord Lovat set off at the head of his 1st Special Service Brigade for the bridges held by the paratroops at Bénouville and Ranville.

At Ouistreham at around 09.30, the Frenchmen of the Kieffer Commando captured the casino, which had

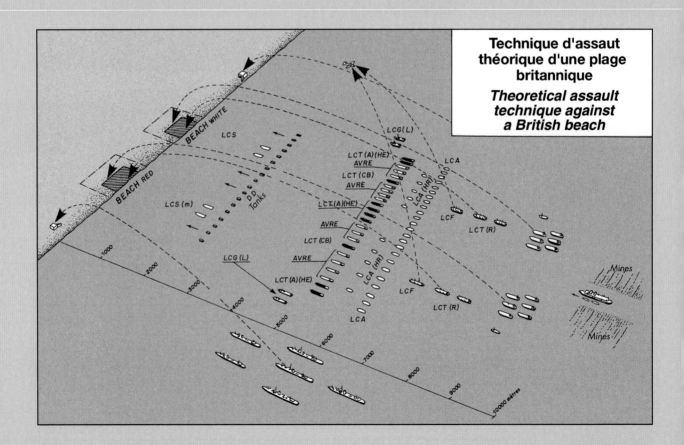

Technique d'assaut théorique d'une plage britannique

Theoretical assault technique against a British beach

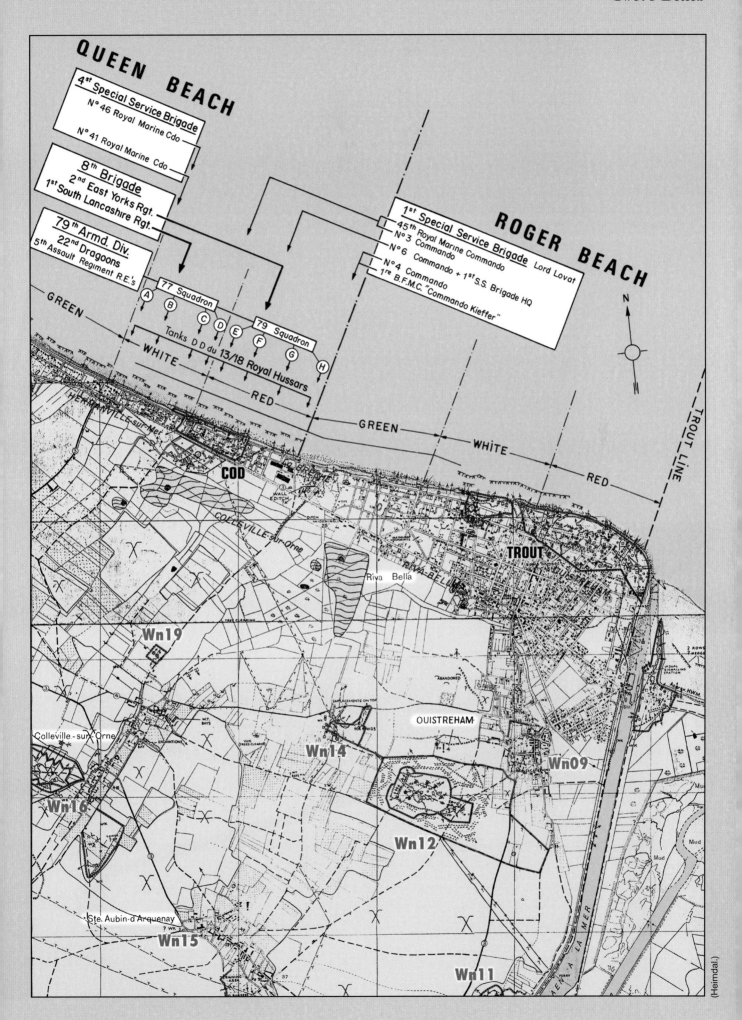

QUEEN BEACH

4ˢᵗ Special Service Brigade
Nᵒ 46 Royal Marine Cdo
Nᵒ 41 Royal Marine Cdo

8ᵗʰ Brigade
2ⁿᵈ East Yorks Rgt.
1ˢᵗ South Lancashire Rgt.

79ᵗʰ Armd. Div.
22ⁿᵈ Dragoons
5ᵗʰ Assault Regiment R.E.'s

ROGER BEACH

1ˢᵗ Special Service Brigade Lord Lovat
45ᵗʰ Royal Marine Commando
Nᵒ 3 Commando
Nᵒ 6 Commando + 1ˢᵗ S.S. Brigade HQ
Nᵒ 4 Commando
1ʳᵉ B.F.M.C. "Commando Kieffer"

GREEN

77 Squadron

79 Squadron

WHITE

Tanks D D du 13/18 Royal Hussars

RED

N

Ⓐ Ⓑ Ⓒ Ⓓ Ⓔ Ⓕ Ⓖ Ⓗ

GREEN   WHITE   RED   TROUT LINE

HERMANVILLE-sur-Mer

COD

COLLEVILLE-sur-Orne

RIVA-BELLA

TROUT

Riva Bella

Wn19

Colleville-sur-Orne

Wn14

OUISTREHAM

Wn09

Wn16

Wn12

Ste. Aubin-d'Arquenay

Wn15

Wn11

(Heimdal.)

been turned into a bunker. At 10.00, Commando n°
4 reached the canal locks, which had not been mined.
The main body of 1st Special Service Brigade carried
on southwards along the Caen ship canal. At around
13.00, accompanied by Bill Millin and the French commandos and followed by the other commandos of the
brigade, Lord Lovat joined Major Howard's men at
Bénouville Bridge, thereby completing the link-up with
the airborne bridgehead. Mission accomplished (see
chapter "Bénouville-Ranville").

To the west, 3rd Infantry Division now had its 185th
Brigade, which mustered in the north of Hermanville at 10.30. Two hours later, Brigadier Smith finally
set off towards Caen with 600 men from three of his
brigade's battalions. On the German side, no counter-attack had got underway so far. Most of the companies of 716. Infanterie-Division were in position
along the coast, and most of them had been wiped
out. Apart from strongpoint "Hillman", little remained
to oppose the advance. The only armored reserve in
the sector was made up of 21.Panzer-Division whose
headquarters were at Saint-Pierre-sur-Dives and its
tank regiment in that same sector, away from the
coast. Although it did however have a few battalions
in the Caen sector, the division was first committed
against the airborne bridgehead east of the Orne, at

06.45. The decision to engage it north of Caen as well did not come through until 10.35. This led the division to be arranged into three battlegroups; one (Kampfgruppe Luck) to fight the paratroops on the east bank of the Orne, the two others (Kampfgruppe Rauch and Kampfgruppe von Oppeln) to be committed on the west bank north of Caen, with orders to move up to the coast, near Lion-sur-Mer for KG Rauch, and between east of Lion and the mouth of the Orne for KG von Oppeln. Unfortunately they could not be engaged until 16.00! The Germans had no clear picture of their plight and their mobile forces were scattered. However, although for several hours 185th Brigade faced practically no further opposition, it failed to capitalize on the situation.

1. *Sergeant Jimmy Mapham, who left Gosport on LCT 610, took this photo as he arrived on Red Beach at H + 35 (08.00 hours) with elements of the 27th Armoured Brigade. On the left, an LCT in flames.*

2. *Another photo by Sergeant Mapham opposite Red Beach showing an AFV burning in front of the villas.*

3. *On this third photo from the same reportage, a Flail tank is burning up on the beach. On the left, a Bobbin tank can be seen waiting for a passage to be cut through the dunes for it to roll out its carpet.*

3

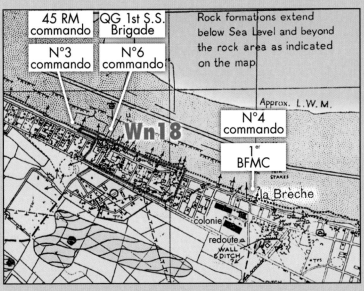

45 RM commando
QG 1st S.S. Brigade
N°3 commando
N°6 commando

Rock formations extend below Sea Level and beyond the rock area as indicated on the map

Approx. L.W.M.

Wn18

N°4 commando

1er BFMC

la Brèche

colonie

redoute

WALL & DITCH

6

5

1. This photo by Sergeant G. Lowe shows N° 4 Commando NCOs preparing grenades on the LCT bringing them onto Queen Red.

2 and **3.** Here now is a reportage by Captain Leslie Evans who was on LCI 519 with Lord Lovat and Bill Millin. From the landing craft's quarterdeck, the 200th Flottilla can be seen advancing across the Channel.

4. LCI 519 now arrives off the beach clluttered with 13th/18th Hussars B Squadron DD tanks opposite the Maison de la Mer (now between the Rue de Pont-l'Evêque and the Rue de l'Amiral Courbet).

5. Lord Lovat has just come ashore (he can be seen on his men's right), and in the right foreground, Bill Millin with his rucksack gets ready to land.

1. *Bill Millin in 1994 playing on the spot where he came ashore.*

2 and 3. *The Commandos of 1st S.S. Brigade are now in the sand dunes opposite the holiday camp.*

4. *They move off inland. Behind them, an AVRE has deployed an SBG bridge.*

5. *In the ruins of the holiday camp.*

3

5

1. Aerial view of La Brèche d'Hermanville, the seaside resort located in front of the old village, White Beach. Lane 7 and Lane 8 are marked on this photo, as are Road 12 and Road 11 respectively. The main square (8/11) is clearly visible. This square appears in most of the pictures shown here. In a line with the square is the road leading to the village of Hermanville.

2 and **3.** While South Lancs A Company has carried on towards Lion-sur-Mer, the men and vehicles of the 9th and 185th Brigades muster near Hermanville before pursuing their advance. Here we see some of the men and vehicles moving eastwards along the coast road (then the N 814 road) towards the main square visible in the background. The jeep belongs to 9th Brigade HQ. (IWM.) This road has changed little, but is now out of the traffic. (HDL.)

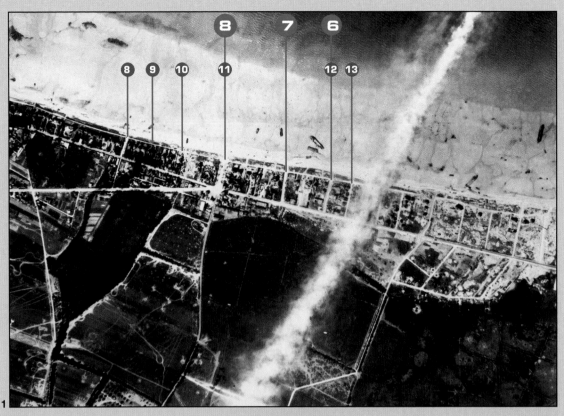

1

2

3

4 and **5.** Sergeant Mapham advances along this street and reaches the square with the Hôtel de la Brèche on the left, and a large villa on the right. A wire entanglement has been pushed back onto the verge. (IWM.) The place has remained the same. (HDL.)

4

5

6

7

10

8

9

6 and **7.** He is now moving into the square. The signpost marked « 94 » shows the way to 185th Brigade's HQ. (IWM & HDL.)

8 and **9.** Turning round, he shows us the frontage of the villa in front of which a Petard AVRE of 77th Assault Squadron going by the name Bulldog is parked. (IWM & HDL.)

10. In memory of this, an AVRE with the name Bulldog painted on it has been placed close by.

Elements of the 6th Airborne Division had landed in the night. Major John Howard seized the Bridges at Ranville, 5th Parachute Brigade landed near Ranville, the 3rd Brigade seized the Merville Battery and the bridge at Troarn.

246 gliders tugged by as many aircraft brought in the bulk of 6th Airlanding Brigade and the heavier equipment 6th Airborne Division so urgently needed. The take-off began around 1850hours, by which time the weather was making a definite improvement. The flights passed off smoothly, although one of the gliders, carrying Lieutenant Geoffrey Sneezum of A Company, the Devonshires, was a little overloaded by a portly war correspondent...

Opposite : Two giant Hamilcars are coming into land on Landing Zone N. 30 such gliders arrived around 21 hours, bring in precious heavy equipment like the 17-pounder anti-tank gun, and light Tetrarch tanks. (IWM)

Most of the coastal German strongpoints were destroyed or taken in the evening of D-Day. But the Germans are bringing troops for a counter-attack, mostly Panzer-Divisions (tanks), but late. So the 12th SS-Panzer-Division « Hitlerjugend » will attack west of Caen, only the 7th June evening.

1. The Panzer IV "536" of the Hitlerjugend rolling for the front on the 6 June. (Heimdal Coll.)

2. One "grenadier" of the "Hitlerjugend" (Hitler Youth) Division. His Regiment will attack in the area of Ardenne Abbey on 7 June. He wear a powerfull Machine-Gun (MG 42). The very young soldiers of this division will fight fiercely. (Heimdal Coll.)

3. Seldom colour picture of a soldier from the "Hitlerjugend" Division. The German soldiers will fight with a very strong determination, the Battle of Normandy will last many weeks with high casualties for the Allies, and also for the Germans. (Heimdal Coll.)

© Editions Heimdal 2009 / 3e édition 2015
Achevé d'imprimer en mai 2015
sur les presses de l'Imprimerie Champagne (Langres, 52), pour le compte des Editions Heimdal